Simple Steps to Reach Each Child Now
Leave No Child without Christ

Ella M. Wade

Literacy IN MOTION

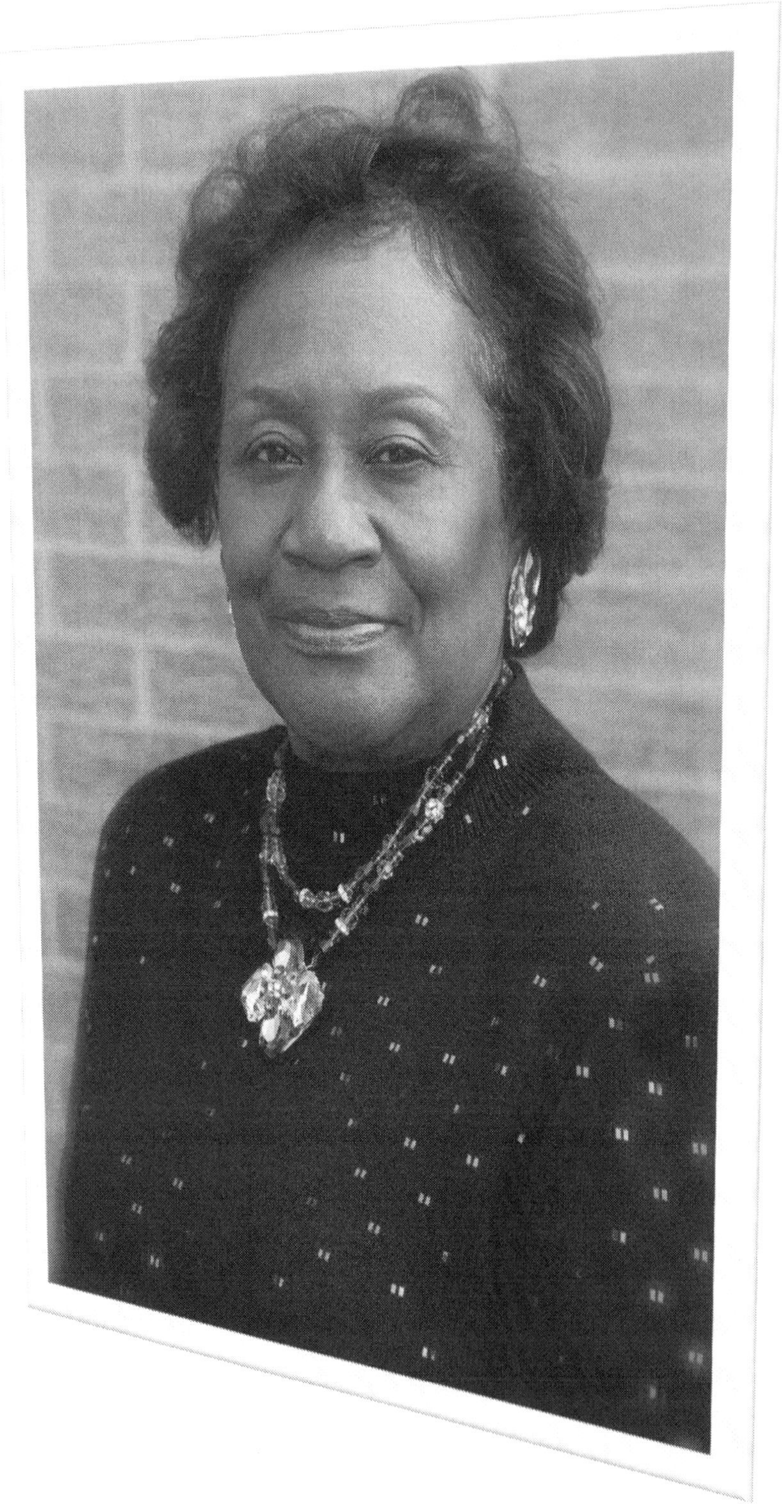

Copyright 2014 by Ella M. Wade
Published by Literacy in Motion

All rights reserved. No portion of this book may be reproduced, scanned, stored in a retrieval system, transmitted in any form or by any means – electronic, mechanical, photocopy, recording, or any other – except for brief quotations in printed reviews without written permission of the publisher. Please do not participate in or encourage piracy of copyrighted materials in violation of the author's rights. Purchase only authorized editions.

Ella M. Wade
Simple Steps to Reach Each Child Now

ISBN: 978-0-9904440-2-2
Christians – Religious Life.
Library of Congress Cataloging in-Publication Data
Printed in the United States of America

Anthony KaDarrell Thigpen, Publisher/Editor-in-Chief
    Monice Johnson-Lillie, Co-Editor

Materials Provided by KLB Publishing

For further information contact:
Literacy in Motion Publishing
www.literacyinmotion.com
6212 US Hwy 6, Suite #232
Portage, IN 46368

PO BOX 11892
Merrillville IN 46411
posttribune@hotmail.com
akthigpen@literacyinmotion.com

Dedication

Every pastor and congregation should know
that children bring new life and growth in the
church. You will receive the blessings of growth
and longevity if you invest in a children's ministry.
God did it for us, and with God you can do it as well.

Table of Contents

Foreword, pg. 6
Acknowledgements, pg. 10
Introduction, pg. 13

Chapter 1, pg. 17
The Lifeline of a Children's Ministry
Chapter 2, pg. 29
Foundations of a Children's Ministry
Chapter 3, pg. 34
How to Develop a Growing Children's Ministry
Chapter 4, pg. 42
**Recruiting through Outreach,
Maintaining through In-Reach**
Chapter 5, pg. 57
How to Motivate Children
Chapter 6, pg. 66
Methods of Teaching Children
Chapter 7, pg. 72
Qualifications and Requirements of Workers
Chapter 8, pg. 79
Persuading Parents to Participate (The 3 P's)
Chapter 9, pg. 89
**The Sustainability of Workers:
Staying with a Children's Ministry**
Chapter 10, pg. 93
A Tribute to Greatness
Chapter 11, pg. 107
Generations Speaks

About the Author, pg. 114

Foreword

All of us have been given gifts by the power and ministry of the Holy Spirit, for the edification of the Body of Christ. God has given to Mrs. Ella Wade the gift of a Children's Ministry. It had been my experience to watch Mrs. Ella Wade with the gift that God has given her to minister to children; to help shape, mold, develop, and esteem children for the Glory of God and for the salvation of their souls.

I thank God for the effective, efficient, and efficacious way in which she has been laborious in this part of the moral vineyard. There are no words to express our gratitude for what God has done through and for this humble servant of God. She stands on the principles of God's word; her faith is in Jesus Christ; her life is surrounded in prayer; and her spirit is satiated with the Holy Spirit. As your husband, our home is the center of your ministry; and as a woman of alphabetical excellence I will praise you, our children arise and call you blessed.

"Many daughters have done virtuously, but thou excellest them all." Proverbs 31:29

Yours for the Cause of Christ,

Rev. Dr. James C. Wade Jr., Pastor Emeritus

Zion Missionary Baptist Church of

East Chicago, Indiana

"Virtuous: Having or showing moral goodness or righteousness" Proverbs 31:10

Mrs. Ella Wade is a great example of a virtuous woman. She strives to live a life of righteousness that pleases God. The love Mrs. Ella M. Wade has for children are like that of Jesus. When Jesus told the disciples in Matthew 19:14, *"But Jesus said, "Suffer little children, and forbid them not, to come unto me: for of such is the kingdom of God."*

She has given her heart, hand, and even her home to make the life of someone stronger in their walk with the Lord. As the Pastor of Zion Missionary Baptist Church, I am truly blessed to have Mrs. Ella Wade on the staff as the Executive Consultant to the Music Ministry. Mrs. Wade's wisdom, talent and hard work are a blessing to the ministry of our church.

Signed By

Rev. Dr. Charles L. Thompson, Jr., Pastor

Zion Missionary Baptist Church of

East Chicago, Indiana

One of the silent words of our day is the term "paradigm." Simply put, the term "paradigm" means "example." I mention the term "paradigm" because I see Mrs. Ella Wade as a "paradigm" for children ministry; particularly, the Children's Music Ministry. Before the term "paradigm" became popular, Mrs. Ella Wade had a business model and mission to implement a powerful Children's Music Ministry.

Mrs. Wade has been able to retain a children's choir of 100 plus since 1986. We were aware that a children's choir is always evolving because children are always moving into their teen years. However Mrs. Wade has been able to maintain the consistency of 100 plus in spite of children moving into their teen years. Mrs. Wade's husband Rev. Dr. J.C. Wade Jr., Dr. Joel Gregory and I have sought to persuade Mrs. Wade to put in writing what God has given her as keys, to building and maintaining a children's music ministry.

Mrs. Ella M. Wade has been challenged to write because she understands that she has been endowed to be a conduit of blessing and not a righteous reservoir. It is my prayer that what will be written will be an axiomatic paradigm for Christian Church Children's Music Ministry.

A Letter from Dr. Melvin Wade Sr.

Mount Moriah Baptist Church

Los Angeles, CA

For decades Mrs. Ella M. Wade of the Zion Missionary Baptist Church in East Chicago, Indiana has led an amazing program with a 100 Voice Children's Choir. Under the supportive guidance of her distinguished Pastor and husband Rev. Dr. James Commodore Wade, Jr., this choir has become a major outreach to the city and beyond. As a frequent speaker at the church, I have been captivated by the children's choir program. One of its amazing marks is the continuity through generations. There are now previous adult members that assist the choir. This book is a practical, step-by-step program that will lead anyone desiring to implement such a choir program for children. The book is born out of decades of experience, as well as practical insights in dealing with children and workers that make the choir a success. I recommend it to Christian workers of all denominations.

A Letter from Joel C. Gregory

Professor of Preaching, George W. Truett Theological Seminary, Baylor University

Distinguished Fellow, Georgetown College

Acknowledgements

To my husband, Rev. Dr. James Commodore Wade, Jr., Pastor Emeritus of Zion Missionary Baptist Church, Thank you for encouraging me to share the blessings we have received by having a Children's Ministry with others. I thank God for giving you the vision, and I thank you for asking me to be a part of the vision. During these 28 years of service we prayed that God would manifest your vision. As we partnered together with the vision in mind, we prayed day and night. God heard our prayers and made it a reality. To God be the Glory forever; all the honor and praise belong to our Lord and Savior Jesus Christ. As noted in the vision, you are an inspiration to me, and our entire church family.

To my children, Rev. James C. Wade III; Mrs. Camellia P. McKinley; and Mrs. LaShonta J. Thompson, you have played a vital part in the Children's Ministry as members who used your talents as instruments to praise God. I thank God for you and for the talents He has given you.

To my present pastor, Rev. Dr. Charles L. Thompson Jr.: How we thank God for you and for how the Lord is using you at Zion Missionary Baptist Church. "Let's take this mountain for we are well able to overcome it" (Numbers 13:30).

To my grandchildren and my great grandchild, God has allowed me to live and to witness you as part of the history of the 100-Plus Voice Children's Choir Ministry. I am eternally grateful. Never forget Jesus.

To My Sister, Mrs. Alice Faye Stanton: Thank you for all the wonderful and memorable years we shared together at home and abroad. You have always supported me in everything and in everyway. Your prayers, advise and special talks will always be cherished, you are my only sister and best friend. Love you Sis.

To Rev. Dr. Melvin V. Wade Sr: Thank you for letting me know that this ministry is not something that you see or witness every day. It was a vision that needed to be manifested. I have not forgotten your prophetic message and I am grateful for your encouraging words.

To Dr. Joel Gregory: Thank you for the words of encouragement and for letting me know that the world needs to know about this awesome ministry that you and Mrs. Gregory witnessed at Zion Missionary Baptist Church.

To the Children's Ministry Workers: Words cannot express the love and thanks I have for you. I thank God for your dedication and faithfulness to serve the Children's Ministry. We have grown closer to the Lord by our acts of valor, and have succeeded in creating a productive and efficient environment. Thank you for the loving care with which you ministered with our precious children.

To Mrs. Pearlie Eatman and the Zion Baptist Church Intercessors: A special thank you for praying for the Children's Ministry and for lifting up every need. I would like to personally thank you for calling me every day for prayer. Continue to pray for us because it is the key in building the kingdom of God.

To Ericka Ware and Vanesha Cook (Armor Bearers), thank you for assisting me with my personal needs. May God continue to bless you. To Mrs. Anne Harrell Wilson: I can never thank you enough for your input to this book.

To the children: You are special. I pray that you learn to develop a relationship with Jesus and that you tell other children about His sacrifice and resurrection. Always remember that the lips of those that love Him spread the gospel. Continue to spread the Gospel.

To the Zion Missionary Baptist Church Family: Thank you for all of your support, commitment, prayers, financial contributions, and dedication in helping the Children's Ministry. Your continuous support is appreciated and we are grateful to God for a church that believes and receives what God has given to the man of God.

Thanks to Kelvin Bride of KLB Publishing. To my editor, Mrs. Monice Johnson-Lillie and my publisher, Anthony KaDarrell Thigpen of Literacy in Motion, I am grateful for your hard work to restore the heart of my message to this book. Thank you and God bless you.

"For God so loved the world that he gave his only begotten Son, that whosoever believeth in Him should not perish, but have ever lasting life." St. John 3:16
I humbly dedicate this book to you in total adoration.

Introduction

We live in perilous times where the enemy is waging war against our cities, communities, and most importantly our children. Our mission is to target ministries that focus on community outreach programs with the intent to strengthen and support families and their children.

Growing up as a young girl I lived with my grandparents, Eliza and Charlie Turner. I had to attend Sunday School, Morning Worship, Baptist Training Union, sing in the choir, play the piano, travel with the church when told, and perform many other church related responsibilities. My mama said, "This was the Lord's Day," and going to church was a requirement, not a debate or question.

Because of the experience I received from my grandparents, I can say today that I am truly grateful for the Christian life and examples they set before me. I have a greater appreciation for them and for life. At New Hope Baptist Church in Daingerfield, Texas where Rev. Otis Warren was pastor, I accepted Jesus as my personal Savior. By being introduced to Christ, I knew that I had received the greatest blessing that I could ever receive: becoming a born again Christian. This is the blessing that every child needs.

Many children today have parents that have not accepted Christ as their Savior, and because many of them don't go to church, the Gospel of Jesus Christ is probably rarely discussed in their homes. A life without the knowledge and understanding of Christ is detrimental to a child's spiritual development. I was blessed to have a family that knew the Lord and to have Aunt Annie Maude, who drove us to church every Sunday. She sometimes had to make two and three trips to ensure everyone made it to church on time. Those important lessons on Christian stewardship, commitment, and sacrifice would be significant in preparing me for what the Lord had in store for me with the 100-PlusVoice Children's Choir.

In 1982, the Lord gave our pastor, Rev. Dr. James Commodore Wade, Jr., a vision to have a 100 Voice Children's Choir. Obeying God's vision, Pastor Wade received confirmation to implement the vision through God's word in Proverbs 29:18, *"Where there is no vision the people perish."* And because he trusted God, his vision to have a Children's Ministry was manifested.

The Lord placed on Pastor Wade's heart to ask me, his loving wife, to lead it. Yes, I prayed about it. My prayer was not whether to accept the challenge, but it was for God to prepare me to lead such a great ministry. I prayed that the Lord would reveal ideas and open doors that would help make this Children's Choir Ministry what He wanted it to be.

As Pastor Wade and I partnered together on the idea, we prayed that the Lord would give me the love and patience to help each child. We vowed to never make a difference between children, and to give every child the opportunity to participate in other opportunities presented. We prayed to show every child that they were important, and that we graciously valued their commitment. Most importantly, we wanted to present the Gospel of Jesus Christ in a way that ensured NO child's soul would be lost.

The vision was fulfilled in 1986. For over thirty-two years, we have been blessed with over 100 children every week. I thank God for Rev. Dr. J.C. Wade, Jr. in giving me the opportunity to serve as director. God blessed the Children's Ministry at Zion Missionary Baptist Church; and we give all the glory to God.

All children deserve a chance to know Jesus. As born again Christians, it is our primary responsibility to ensure that their minds are conformed to the ideology that articulates they are a blessing from the Lord.

As stated in the lyrics of the timeless song, *Jesus Loves the Little Children,*

"Jesus loves the little children, all the children of the world. Red and yellow, black and white, they are precious in His sight. Jesus loves the little children of the world."

We must teach our children "The Plan of Salvation" which confirms that God loves them and offers a wonderful plan for their lives. We must ourselves individually receive Jesus Christ as Savior and Lord. Only then can we gain the wisdom and spiritual discernment that assure God's love and plan for our lives.

Simple Steps to Reach Each Child Now is written for the sole purpose of teaching you how to reach children at home and abroad through a Children's Ministry, which embodies the physical, cultural, economic, and spiritual development of every child.

Chapter 1:
The Lifeline of a Children's Ministry

There will never be enough children until every child is saved. Children are waiting for someone to tell them about Jesus, and it is our responsibility to get the message to them about our Lord and Savior Jesus Christ. We face the following challenges with our children today:

- children that are kidnapped, missing and never found;
- children that are abused, molested and victims of incest;
- children that are killed by drive-by shootings, in fires and in wars;
- children that are on the streets, homeless, hungry and naked;
- children that are left on doorsteps, home alone or placed in foster care;
- children that are not loved;
- children that are born with addictions or become addicted themselves to drugs and alcohol;
- children that drop out of school or become teen parents;
- children that do not know their parents;
- children that are afflicted with AIDS and other diseases;
- children that become juvenile delinquents;
- children that don't go to church; and
- children that are unsaved

We MUST reach out with compassion and love to help lead these children into a saving knowledge of Jesus Christ.

In the Beginning
100-Voice Children's Choir Since 1982

On many occasions in the Bible we see God commanding His people to "tell their children and their children's children. It is important to God that we pass on His love and provisions through Jesus Christ to EVERY generation. The Zion Missionary Baptist Church 100-Plus Voice Children's Choir has been singing praises to the Lord from generation to generation, and they continue to do so.

Shortly after the confirmation of the vision for the 100 Voice Children's Choir, rehearsals began. The assignment for second Sunday was placed on this newly formed children's choir in 1982. Since then, the 100 Voice Children's choir still sings on the second Sunday of every month. They have never missed their monthly assignment of giving praises through song, dance, mime, drill teams and much more. The choir began with songs such as *"I Do Believe," "If You're Happy and You Know It Say Amen," "Deep,"* and *"Lift Him Up."* Over 20 years ago the children began to sing in 3-part-harmony, no longer in unison.

In 1983, the First Anniversary of the 100 Voice Children's Choir was held on the second Sunday in March. The anniversary celebration has continued every year, except in 1999 when our pastor, Rev. Dr. J.C. Wade, Jr., was standing in the gap for his brother with a bone morrow transplant and Mrs. Ella Wade was at his side.

In 1986 the vision that was given by God to Rev. Dr. J.C. Wade, and led by Mrs. Ella Wade was realized when 104 children participated in the Fourth Anniversary. By the 19th Anniversary, the name had changed to the 100-Plus Voice Children's Choir.

In 2001, at the 19th Anniversary, the 100-Plus Voice Children's Choir recorded their first album, *"Save the Children,"* produced by Elder Clarence "Maxx" Frank with original music written by Mrs. Ella Wade and Elder Frank.

When the 100-voice plus Children's Choir began, children joined at the age of five and stayed until they were 13 or 14 years old. A few stayed even longer as junior workers, helping with the younger choir members. When children turned 13 years old, they had the option to serve as junior workers or move to the teen choir.

Children can now join the choir at the age of two years old; however, they must be potty trained. At the choir's 29th Anniversary Celebration, approximately 21 children were five years old or younger.

During the 28th Anniversary a DVD was made of the 100 Plus Voice Children's Choir, even sound, etc. The videographer was so enthralled with what he saw that he remained the entire evening.

Children Ministry Workers

When Mrs. Ella Wade started the ministry, she had seven committed workers: Brooksie Buggs, Evelyn Forte, Shirley Hall, Deana Johnson, Rubye Pruitt, Freddie Upshaw and the-late Ms. Ida Marie Hood (worker Emeritus). For over 28 years, 36 women and three men have toiled in the vineyard of the 100-Plus Voice Children's Choir. On many occasions, Deana Johnson would direct the choir when Mrs. Ella Wade had to play the organ for other services.

For 27 years, Sis. Yvonne Sanders, better known as "My member" has been a true worker and servant helping with the 100-Plus Voice Children's Choir. The children call her "Miss Cool Whip" because she is a disciplinary. Sis Loris Bradford, another faithful worker for over 26 years, is still dedicated to the 100-Plus Voice Children's Choir. For 12 years, Mrs. Camellia P. McKinley served as a worker and assistant director to Mrs. Ella Wade.

She taught songs, as well as directed, the Children's Choir. Mrs. Lashonta Thompson worked with Mrs. Wade and the children's choir as assistant director for two years.

Passing the Torch

In 2010, after 28 years of leadership, Mrs. Wade turned over the helm of the 100 Plus Voice Children's Choir to Mrs. LaShonta Thompson, her daughter and the new First Lady of Zion Missionary Baptist Church.

Under the leadership of our new pastor, Rev. Dr. Charles L. Thompson, Jr., we look forward to the continuation of this vision.

Our Showcase of Stars

Although famous guests like Deleon Richards have participated in the 100-Plus Voice Anniversaries, the most memorable celebrations have featured our own showcase of stars, the 100-Plus Voice Children's Choir. They were featured in plays: *"Bridge Over Trouble Waters"* written by Pat Dixon-Darden; *"Somebody's Watching You," "Miracles of Jesus," "Noah's Ark,"* and *"Zion's Idol's,"* all written by Mrs. Wade. Sandra Hoggs, Dorothy Smith, Rosie Ivy, Sharon Scott, Minnie Hunter and other members created elaborate costumes. Mrs. Wade has written original songs for each production.

Fact: "The Majority of Christian Ministers came to Christ as Children"

One night I was awakened from my sleep with the lyrics and tune to this song, *"Save the Children."* I began to write these words and hum the tune. It blessed me more than you will ever know. Just as I was blessed, my desire was for others to be blessed and inspired to help "Save the Children."

"Save the Children"

We need the Lord, to save the children

Lord to save the Children

Lord to save the Children

O Lord save the children, save us all

And the Lord God formed man out of the dust of the ground

Breathed into his nostrils the breath of life

And man became a living soul (repeat)

O Lord, save the children save us all

No Matter how large or small

Great or tall, God has the power

Because He made us all

O, Lord to save the Children

O, Lord to save the Children

O, Lord to save the Children

Save us all

Since 1982, over 3000 children and four generations have participated in the 100-Plus Voice Children's Choir. In 2001, 167 children participated in the 100-Plus Voice Children's Choir. That year we had the largest number to ever participate. We thank God for blessing our pastor with such a vision, and for allowing me to work faithfully beside him and so many others in seeing it come alive. To God be the Glory for the things He has done.

Why Have A Children's Ministry?

Recently, I came across a report from Oak Park to the Ends of the Earth: God's Plan for Calvary Memorial Church called *"One Day in the Lives of America's Children"* According to this report, every day in the USA:

- 2,995 teens get pregnant
- 372 teens miscarry
- 1,106 teens have abortions
- 1, 295 teens give birth
- 27 children die from poverty
- 10 children are killed by guns
- 30 children are wounded by guns
- 6 teenagers commit suicide
- 135,000 children bring a gun to school
- 7, 742 teenagers become sexually active
- 625 teenagers get syphilis or gonorrhea
- 211 children are arrested for drugs abuse
- 437 children are arrested for drinking or for drunken driving

- 1,512 teens drop out of school
- 1,849 children are abused or neglected
- 3,288 children run away from home
- 1,629 children are in adult jails
- 2,556 children are born out of wedlock
- 2,989 children see their parents divorced

> **There are roughly 2.4 million people in prison. There are 1,719 state prisons, 102 federal prisons, 2,259 juvenile correctional facilities, and 3,283 local jails. Our prisons are filled mainly with men under age 40, with Blacks and Hispanics accounting for more than half of its population.**

Children deserve a chance to know that there is a God who has all power in His hands. He sent his Son Jesus who suffered, bled and died for the sins of the world. If you can believe it, receive it, accept it and confess it; you can have it. And that's "Eternal Life."

Romans 10: 8, 9, 10 says, *"But what saith it? The word is nigh thee, even in thy mouth, and in thy hear: that is, the word of faith which we preach; That if thou shalt confess with thy mouth the Lord Jesus, and shalt believe in thine heart that God hath raised him from the dead, thou shalt be saved. For with the heart man believeth unto righteousness; and with the mouth confession is made unto salvation".*

Why Have a Children's Ministry?

We simply cannot afford not to have one. How many children do you know who fall into one or more of these categories? The lyrics in Yolanda Adams' song, "*What about the Children,*" highlights the current situation of our children and youth and the urgent need for us to act.

> Tears streaming down, her heart is broken
> And because her heart is hurting, so am I
> He wears a frown, his dreams are choking
> And because he stands alone, his dreams will die
> So, humbly I come to you and I say
> As I sound aloud the warfare of today
> Please hear me, I pray
>
> [CHORUS]
> What about the children
> To ignore is so easy
> So many innocent children will choose the wrong way
> So what about the children
> Remember when we were children

And if not, for those who loved us and who cared enough to show us

Where would we be today?

So, where is your son?

And where lies his refuge

And if that young man can't come to you, then where can that

Young man run to

She's such a foolish foolish girl, yet still, she's your daughter

And if you will just reminisce on all the crazy things that you did when you were that young

You see, it's not where you've been, nor what you've done

Because I know a friend who specializes in great outcomes

See His love overcomes

[CHORUS]

What about the children

To ignore is so easy

So many innocent children will choose the wrong way

So what about the children

Remember when we were children

And if not, for those who loved us and who cared enough to show us

Where would we be today?

What about the children they need our help today
And what about the children they need us
More than ever more than ever more then ever
What about the children where would we be today
Where would we be today?
What about the children

Where would we be today?
Where would we be today?
Where would we be today?
What about the children

- Yolanda Adams

Chapter 2:
Foundation of a Children's Ministry

The world is in such a state that children's ministry is critical and these ministries must have solid foundations.

Merriam-Webster defines *Foundation* as, *"A basis upon which something stands or is supported."* As Christians, we know that Jesus Christ is that foundation; and all that we do in our Children's Ministry must be built on that "solid foundation,"

Kim Williams. Director of Pre-School Ministries at First Baptist Church, Woodstock, GA. writes about the four sources for connecting a Children's Ministry to the foundation of Jesus Christ.

Connect to the Center

The center of a child's life is the adult who cares for him day by day.

Connect to the Core

The core of an individual is their eternal capacity: Their soul.

Connect to the Community

The community of a church is the tangible location and the individual who lives and works there should not be untouched by that church.

Connect to the Commission

There is a purpose for the church being established. It is stated in the Scripture. (Matthew 28:18-20)

I'd like to add a fifth connection, which I believe is also significant to the foundation of a Children's Ministry.

Connect to the Church

The church is a source for connecting to the foundation through the fellowship of believers. The church is significant in the development of a child's religious experiences. Many parents have accepted Jesus Christ as their Savior through their own children's experiences in church.

Rev. Dr. Harry Blake Sr., Pastor of Mt. Canaan Baptist Church in Shreveport, Louisiana said, "We must lay a solid foundation." He emphasizes the importance of having a solid foundation and sound strategy.

5 Steps Needed to Building a Solid Foundation

Step 1. Visualize - See the need
Step 2. Prioritize - The need
Step 3. Organize - For the need
Step 4. Revitalize - The need
Step 5. Publicize - The need

We Must Develop a Sound Strategy

1. **Find them:** To locate or recover, to come up on by chance, something lost and replaced.

2. **Fetch them:** To go after and bring back, return with, get, to cause to come

3. **Feed them:** To give food to, supply with nourishment, to provide what is necessary for the existence or the development of, to eat.

4. **Fence them:** To guard, protect, surround

Church membership is not a prerequisite to participation in the ministry. It is through this ministry that children will be taught the plan of salvation and accept Jesus as their personal Savior.

Below is a list of rules and mandates that should be considered when implementing your Children's Ministry.

The children have to follow the requirements listed below to be a part of the Children's Ministry.
- Attend Sunday School
- Attend, and be on time, for choir rehearsals
- Be obedient at all times
- No eating food or chewing gum in the sanctuary

- Listen to adults for direction
- Do not leave the rehearsal at any time without permission
- Absolutely no fighting
- No use of inappropriate language
- No bad attitudes
- Memorize scriptures
- Memorize the books of the Bible - Old and New Testament
- Learn to pray and take part in prayer
- Take an active part in all programs as well as every second Sunday Worship
- Participate when asked to sing for other services or outings
- Wear proper uniform
- Give the director and workers respect and undivided attention
- Listen and follow the choir director
- Respect the Pastor
- Respect the Lord's house at all times

Chapter 3:
How to Develop a Growing Children's Ministry

A Children's Ministry must be carefully developed. Below are seven ways to develop a Children's Ministry. It begins with the Pastor and Leaders.

I. Pastors and leaders must have an insatiable thirst and desire to produce a Children's Ministry.

II. Pastors and leaders must be willing to pray for a powerful and productive Children's Ministry. Good Pastors and leaders lead from their knees. The following scriptures stress the importance of why we lead from our knees.

In Jeremiah 33:3, the Bible says, *"Call unto me and I will answer thee, and shew thee great and mighty things, which thou knowest not."* (KJV)

Philippians 4:6, *"Be careful for nothing; but in everything by prayer and supplication with thanksgiving let your requests be known unto God."* (KJV)

I John 5:14, 15,

"And this is the confidence that we have in him, that If we ask any thing according to his will he heareth us. (15) And if we know that he heareth us , whatsoever we ask, we know that we have the petitions that we desired of him." (KJV)

"And we are sure of this, that he will listen to us whenever we ask him for anything in line with his will. (15)And if we really know he is listening when we talk to

him and make our requests, then we can be sure that he will answer us." (LBV)

"We are sure that if we ask anything that He wants us to have, He will hear us. (15) If we are sure He hears us when we ask, we can be sure He will give us what we ask for." (NLV)

Matthew 7:7-8, "Ask, and what you are asking for will be given to you. Look, and what you are looking for you will find. Knock, and the door you are knocking on will be opened to you. (8) Everyone who asks receives what he asks for. Everyone who knocks has the door opened to him." (NLV)

Matthew 21:22, "All things you ask for in prayer, you will receive if you have faith." (NLV)

John 16: 23-24, "When the time comes that you see Me again, you will ask Me no question. For sure, I tell you, My Father will give you whatever you ask in My name. (24) Until now you have not asked for anything in My name. Ask and you will receive. Then you joy will be full." (NLV)

Isaiah 58:9, "Then you will call, and the Lord will answer. You will cry, and He will say, 'Here I am.'" (NLV)

Mark 11:24, "Because of this, I say to you, whatever you ask for when you pray, have faith that you will receive it. Then you will get it." (NLV)

III. Pastors and other leaders must make the Children's Ministry a priority. Matthew 6:33, *"But seek ye first the Kingdom of God and His righteousness, and all these things shall be added unto you."*

IV. Pastors and leaders must develop a plan and strategy for Children's Ministry. II Timothy 2: 14-15, *"Remind you people of these great facts, and command them in the name of the Lord not to argue over unimportant things. Such arguments are confusing and useless and even harmful. (15) Work hard so God can say to you, "Well done." Be a good workman, one who does not need to be ashamed when God examines your work. Know what his Word says and means."* (LBV)

V. Pastors and leaders must be co-laborers together with God. We must have strong positive expectations and avoid Cynicism.

The word *Cynicism* means:
- An attitude of scornful and jaded negativity
- A negative comment or act
- A cynical action, remark or idea
-

VI. Pastors and leaders must avoid delay.
- Offer and accept constructive suggestions
- Give clear directions
- Set and meet deadlines
- Help children identify and solve problems
- Guide the group in goal setting and decision Making
- Delegate responsibilities

- Create a productive atmosphere

VII. Pastors and leaders must be prepared to provide ministry without compromise in this Post Modern Age. Charles Wesley in his song "A Charge to Keep I have," speaks of our charge to fulfill our Master's (God's) will.

A Charge To Keep I Have:

A charge to keep I have,

A God to glorify,

Who gave His Son my soul to save,

And fit it for the sky.

To serve the present age,

My calling to fulfill,

O may it all my pow're engage

To do my Master's will

Gary McIntosh, in his book *Biblical Church Growth*, states that he asked pastors and church leaders the following three questions:

- ✓ **Do you want your church to decline?**
- ✓ **Do you want your church to plateau?**
- ✓ **Do you want your church to grow?**

If you do not want your church to decline or plateau but to grow, then you need to develop a children's ministry. A church with little or no active children's ministry is a dying church.

Persistence is the Key

St Matthews 19:14 says, *"But Jesus said, Suffer little children, and forbid them not, to come unto me: for of such is the kingdom of heaven."* This is one of the scriptures that the children say at choir rehearsal. They must commit it to memory.

When developing a Children's Ministry, those involved must understand that there will be sleepless nights, and situations, which will test their faith and commitment. Whenever those moments occurred with me, I would remember this testimony, which has blessed my life. I like to share it with leaders who are responsible for developing Children's Ministries.

During our Saturday morning outreach, Pastor Wade and I, along with some other workers would knock on doors to invite children to come and join our Children's Ministry at Zion Baptist Church. If we did not get results from certain homes, we would go again and again until something happened.

One particular week, when I knocked on the door of a family the mother said that her children could not participate. I responded, "Okay, thank you." The next Saturday I went again. She came to the door and yelled, "I said they cannot go and don't knock on my door again!" I left with my feelings hurt and felt like giving up although I knew that those children most likely had not been introduced to Jesus. I went home and told Pastor Wade that I had my feelings hurt and I was not going to that house anymore. Of course, he told me to pray before I made the decision because I was dealing with souls. I began to pray. In seeking God's will I learned that you have to be persistent and consistent when you are doing the work of the Lord.

The next Saturday I went back, but I did not knock on that same family's door. I knocked on the neighbor's door next to her apartment. I hit the door with all the strength I had. It was so loud that the mother from the apartment I had previously approached ran to the door and hollered in a loud harsh voice, "Didn't I tell you not to knock on my door," she yelled!" To her surprise, I was knocking on the neighbor's door. She looked at me and said, "I thought you were knocking on my door again." I said "NO!" Her reply was shocking. She said, "Since you have been coming here every Saturday saying the same thing, I am going to let my children come and join Zion Children's Ministry."

I began to thank God. I hugged the lady, signed the children up and they came and accepted Jesus Christ as their personal Savior, and united with our church. This blessed my life tremendously. Never give up on souls because God didn't give up on us. Remember, He gave his life that we might have eternal life.

Chapter 4:
Recruiting through Outreach, Maintaining through In-Reach

The word evangelism comes from the Greek word "euangelion," which simply means "good news." The ultimate goal and purpose of evangelism is to bring the hearer to receive Jesus Christ through faith, that they might align their hearts in the path of righteousness with God.

J.G. McCann Sr., Pastor of St. Luke Baptist Church in Harlem, New York said, "Evangelism is not forcing or imposing the gospel upon someone. The Gospel of Jesus Christ should be presented with love and grace. As the Scriptures declares in Jeremiah 31:3, *'with loving kindness have I drawn you.'* Within the word evangelism is the word 'angel.' An angel by definition is a messenger of God. When a messenger brings a message, he or she does not argue with the recipient or force the message. If one decides not to receive the message, the messenger continues on the next assignment.

Our job as messengers for God is to present the gospel, the good news of Jesus Christ with love, grace and dignity. True evangelism is not compulsive. The fact that the temperature of sin has been turned up in this 21st century, the messenger of the good news must act more aggressively without being forceful. The Holy Spirit teaches the believer who is on divine assignment how to adjust within every scenario."

We must be willing to share Jesus Christ with our children, and want His love for children to be circulating. A bell is not a bell until you ring it. A song is not a song until you sing it. A toy is not a toy until you share it and love is not love until you give it.

The nature of love is such that it cannot be starved; it must be shared. It is through our Outreach Ministry that we share the love of Jesus Christ to our children and parents. Outreach (Evangelism) is the bridge we build between our love for God and our love for others, through the work of the Holy Spirit in us. God can complete his transformation of a person for His purpose and glory. We cannot give away what we don't have. Effective outreach always involves sincere and fervent prayer that God will bless the effort. Romans 5:8 says, *"But God commendeth his love toward us, in that, while we were yet still sinners, Christ died for us."*

The Significance of a Strategy

Pastor Wade and I began with a season of prayer. After praying, he announced the vision of a 100 Voice Children's Choir Ministry to the congregation. A date and time was set for the rehearsals, and a Sunday was designated for the Children to sing. The children would sing the second Sunday of each month with rehearsals set for every Tuesday from 5:30 p.m. to 7:30 p.m.

After the first rehearsals, Pastor Wade and I went out every Saturday following 10:00 a.m. prayer to knock on doors and invite new children to be a part of this ministry. We would always have registration forms, which were to be completed by the children and their parents. Our recruitment strategy included Outreach Ministry, the In-Reach Ministry and the Bus Ministry.

Outreach Registration Form

(Please Print Clearly)

Date: _____

Name_____

Age _____ Gender Male ( ) Female ( )

_____
Street Address   Apartment #

_____
City   State   Zip

( )_____ ( )_____
Contact Numbers / Home   Cellular

Do you have a church home?   If yes, what is the name
Yes [ ]   No [ ]   of your church?

                                _____

For Minors ONLY

_____
Name of Parent(s) or Guardian(s)

Bus Ministry Pick-Up Form

(Please Print Clearly)

Date: _____

Name _____

Age _____   Gender Male ( )   Female ( )

_____
Street Address   Apartment #

_____
City   State   Zip

( )_____ ( )_____
Contact Numbers / Home   Cellular

Rider Age Group (Circle One)

Infant   Child   Teen   Adult

An adult or responsible child must accompany children under 5 years of age.

Pick up Area (Circle One)   E.C.   Gary (West)   Gary (East)

Designated Driver _____

Order of Worship Form
Children's Ministry

This is ONLY an example of the ORDER OF WORSHIP for one particular Sunday service. The order of worship can be with or without a theme.

Entrance into the Sanctuary	Children
Devotion	Children
Broadcast Announcers	Children
Prayer	Children
Scripture	Children
Mission Statement	Children
Vision	Children
Morning Hymn	Children
Announcements	Children
Spoken Word	Pastor
Period of Decision	Pastor
Tithe, Offering and Pastoral Support	Children/Others

Children's Ministry Festival Form

Ministry Event Planning

Time

Place

Flyers

Registration

Menu

Games

Prizes

Workers

The Outreach Ministry
Telling every nation about the goodness of the Lord

Outreach Ministry consists of Christian men and women who have dedicated and committed themselves to go out and witness to those who do not know Christ.

The main purpose of the Outreach Ministry is to encourage children to come to church and accept Christ as their personal Savior. Our prayer is that the children will be an inspiration to their parents who would then be inspired to accept Christ too.

Children have the ability to share Jesus Christ with their parents and peers, like no one else.

Children are some of the best evangelists and soul winners that we have in the church. If you want your church *to grow, go, and get some children!*

Isaiah 11: 6 "...And a little child shall lead them."

St. Luke 14:23: *"Jesus said unto the servant, Go out into the highways and hedges, and compel them to come in, that my house may be filled."*

Tips for a Successful Outreach Ministry

- One of the most effective ways to reach children is by going out and knocking on their

doors.
- Always pray before you go out. The best time to go is in the morning before noon. If it is not a school day, you can usually find children home at this time
- Have your registration forms and flyers ready to present.
- Before you go, do a demographic study of those areas that has a large population of children.
- Go in groups of two or more.
- Be friendly and do not appear nervous.
- Be patient with people when you visit their homes; they may not always receive or welcome you.
- Complete the registration forms accurately.
- Leave a flyer or brochure if there is no answer at the door.
- Return to the church for prayer and report.
- Know the Plan of Salvation yourself

(The 4 Spiritual Laws)

The 4 Spiritual Laws Plus 1

1. God loves you and offers a wonderful plan for your life. (John 3:16, John 10:10).

2. Man is sinful and separated from God. Therefore, he cannot know and experience God's love and plan for his life. (Romans 3:23, Romans 6:23)

3. Jesus Christ is God's only provision for man's sin. Through Him you can know and experience God's love and plan for your life. (Romans 5:8, I Corinthians 15:3- 6, John 14:6).

4. We must individually receive Jesus Christ as Savior and Lord; then we can know and experience God's love and plan for our lives. (John1:12, Ephesians 2:8,9, John 3:1-8, Revelation 3:20).

Plus 1.

Do not be discouraged when people promise to come and do not show.

Thus far I have discussed the importance of your outreach efforts in recruiting children for your Children's Ministry. However, these efforts are futile if you do not have a plan for maintaining children for long-term commitments to ministry work. It makes no sense to pray for the success of your Outreach efforts without also praying for the success of your In-Reach efforts.

The In-Reach Ministry

Our In-Reach Ministry consists of a weekly telethon, ongoing visitations, the Children's Ministry closet, telethon and Bus Ministry. Instead of going out on Saturdays, we make calls through the efforts of our telethon, following up with individuals, and making sure that telephone numbers and addresses are correct for pick up. Be sure to document and update every contact made during outreach and in-reach.

Visitation is a very important part of the In-reach Ministry. Home visits are necessary because with many individuals it is the only way we have for communicating with them.

We make visits to homes when:

- A child or parent has repeatedly missed church
- Phone calls have not been returned
- A child or parent has been delinquent or sick;
- A number has been disconnected
- A child or parent has moved to another location

We come together for prayer at the church and then go out as a group. We go in the name of our Lord and Savior Jesus Christ, to reach out and "reconnect" with our children and parents.

Children's Ministry Closet

It is also our responsibility through the In-Reach Ministry to ensure that our children are equipped with what they need to feel good about participating in the 100-Plus Voice Choir, and other Children's Ministry activities. To make sure all children have what they need to participate in the choir and other activities, we created the Children's Ministry Closet using a room in the church.

There are some children who might not have on the proper uniform for that day. We make sure they have the proper attire so that they can look good, feel loved and feel special just like other children. We also keep an iron and ironing board in the closet to make sure their clothes are neat and presentable. Children participate more willingly when they are able to be in uniform like the other children.

We purchase and receive donations for boys and girls from ages two through 12 years old. Anyone working in a Children's Ministry knows that there will always be children whose parents either cannot afford to buy them what they need, or they are unable to provide. We have always been blessed with members who love sharing in this capacity.

The following items are usually needed for our Children's Ministry Closet:

Girls

Shoes, socks, tights, skirts, blouses, underwear, hair accessories, toiletries, robes, comb & brush, deodorant, safety pins & etc.

Boys

Shoes, socks, pants, shirts, underwear, toiletries, belts, robes, brush, deodorant & etc.

The Bus Ministry (In-Reach and Outreach)

The Bus Ministry was established to pick up and drop off children and workers when transportation is needed.

The church provides the transportation and it has been a blessing to the Children's Ministry for over 32 years.

The Bus Ministry has been an integral part of the success of the 100 Plus Voice Children's Choir. In the beginning, Ms. Grace Alston and Mrs. Alfreda Thompson braved the elements over a large part of Lake County to get the children to rehearsal. For 32 years there have been more than 20 people who have served as bus drivers for the choir.

The bus ministry consists of Christian men and women who have committed and dedicated themselves to drive the bus and pick up people needing this service. To serve on the Bus Ministry each driver must possess and do the following:

- A Born again Christian
- A praying bus driver
- Loves the lord
- Loves the church
- Loves the pastor
- Loves children
- Is dependable
- Have a valid driver's license
- Have a safe driving record
- Have patience
- Is willing to serve and give time
- Is punctual
- Have a scheduled time for pick up and drop off
- Have bus monitors
- NEVER leave a child unsupervised

Dr. W.T. Crutcher, former Pastor of Mt. Olive Baptist Church in Knoxville, Tennessee wrote a guide for National Baptist Churches on the importance of the Bus Ministry as part of the In-Reach and Out-Reach Ministries.

Dr. Crutcher said, "A bus ministry is first and foremost a ministry! Thus, however and wherever bus ministries are implemented this factor must be primary- it is a ministry. And to be true to Scripture, it must express the Biblical concept of ministering.

The words minister and ministry both come from the same word meaning to serve. The Scripture also uses these words in the context of witnessing to the gospel of the Kingdom (Acts 1:8). We serve by leading others to submit themselves to Jesus as Lord and Savior. Thus the bus ministry is a program of using motor vehicles in giving a witness of the Lordship of Christ to persons and families within and beyond the local congregation. It is a ministry of bringing the gospel to people and the people to the gospel.

It is ultimately a ministry of outreach. This is generally viewed as witnessing to the "unchurched" or evangelizing. The bus ministry is a means of taking the gospel to persons needing salvation. It is also a means of bringing them into the fellowship of believers. *To God be the Glory for the things He has done.*

BRING THEM IN!

Mark 10:13-16 says, *"And they brought young children to him, that he should touch them: and his disciples rebuked those that brought them. (14) But when Jesus saw it, he was much displeased, and said unto them, suffer the little children to come unto me, and forbid them not: for of such is the kingdom of God. (15) Verily I say unto you, whosoever shall not receive the kingdom of God as a little child, he shall not enter therein. (16) And he took them up in his arms, put his hands upon them, and blessed them."*

Chapter 5:
How to Motivate Children

They Are Our Future

The Miriam Webster Dictionary defines *motivation* as "to give (someone) a reason for doing something." This is especially true for children. Give them incentives for good behavior and a job well done. You can award them individually or as a group.

Anthony Robbins, a bestselling author on motivation said "Life is a gift, and it offers us the privilege, opportunity, and responsibility to give something back by becoming more."

In a Children's Ministry, you must develop strategies to motivate children, especially with the emphasis on technology today. Be deliberate in developing powerful strategies to keep children learning and involved in ministry.

Motivational Strategies

- Give special treats at the close of rehearsal
- Serve food at the children's workshops
- Plan picnics in the summer
- Award good behavior with double treats
- Plan a fun festival with games, prizes, food and other fun things
- Host a bible quiz contest with prizes
- Hold vocal and instrumental auditions
- Give special recognition certificates and awards presentations
- Plan a talent show

- Allow children to take an active part in planning the programs
- Plan outings for the children

I also recommend implementing motivational ideas for Sunday school. Present trophies to the winning class each Sunday (trophies are to stay at the church). The class that keeps the trophy for the month or quarter should be given a prize or special recognition.

Motivational Ideas

- Attendance (trophy)
- Offering (trophy)
- Bibles (trophy)
- The child who invited the most guest (stickers or ribbons)
- Children who show up on time (pins)
- Treats for the class
- McDonald's gift cards
- Certificates
- Take picture of students and teacher and post on bulletin board
- Announce the winning class in a newsletter
- Fun night to include movies, games, rap session, snacks and basketball
- Summer outings
- Sunday School picnics

"We Have To Produce What We Advertise"

Rev. Melvin Von Wade Sr., Pastor of Mount Moriah Baptist Church, Los Angeles, California tells a story about an experience he had with Rev. Samuel Gilbert II, Pastor of Mount Sanai Baptist Church, Houston, Texas.

One day the two of them went to Church's Chicken to order a "Chicken Special" that had been advertised. When they arrived and placed their order, the server had to apologize for not having the special, which was advertised earlier.

> **Understandably they were disappointed, but oftentimes this is what happens in our churches. We don't produce what we advertise. What a sad indictment.**

Dr. H. Devore Chapman, on the other hand says Chick-fil-A is one of the most talked about food chains in the country for the following reasons:

- They have taken their time to perfect their product over the years.
- They have remained true to their product and have kept their menus small.
- They have a requirement that all owners must be managers first to ensure that the original brand is maintained as franchises grow.

- They have learned to do one thing and do it right.

Is your Children's Ministry like Chick-fil-A or like that Church's Chicken restaurant, which did not produce what they advertised? Unlike Church's Chicken and Chick-fil-A, the product we advertise is too important to neglect because our product is "Eternal Life," through Jesus Christ.

Romans 10:8-10 says, *"But what saith it? The word is nigh thee, even in thy mouth, and in thy heart: that is, the word of faith which we preach; (9) That if thou shalt confess with thy mouth the Lord Jesus, and shalt believe in thine heart that God hath raised him from the dead, thou shalt be saved. (10) For with the heart man believeth unto righteousness; and with the mouth confession is made unto salvation."*

Rev. Dr. Charles L. Thompson Jr. made a powerful statement during one of his sermons when he said, "The answer to our children is not in the electric chair, but in the high chair."

God blesses your ministry with motivated children when you are motivated. Motivated young people do not happen by "osmosis or spontaneous combustion." In other words, it doesn't just happen. First, there must be a special love for children. Next, there must be a commitment to "leave no child without Christ."

Over 51 years in marriage, 50 years as a mother, and 28 years as Director of Children's Ministry, I have experienced the importance of sharing love not only with our children, but with other children as well.

Three children come to mind in my spirit. One is Kabisa, whom we loved as an infant. We fed and clothed Kabisa; she slept with us and went to church with us. We want to keep her as our own.

Another child is Jamal. Jamal was a handsome little boy that we fell in love with. So many weekends he would spend the night with us, especially on Saturday, so he could go to church on Sunday. Again, our family loved Jamal like he was a part of us.

Deana and her daughter Chareice, are received like our daughter and granddaughter. Deana's mother, Ruby Johnson would always say that she never worried about Deana because she was with us, and "in good hands." During Deana's pregnancy some ostracized her. We continued sharing our love for her, nurtured her, and let her know that God still loved her, and we loved her too. We assured Deana that all was not lost and that she could make it despite her circumstance.

Today, Deana is the Administrative Assistant of the Zion Missionary Baptist Church for Rev. Dr. Charles L. Thompson, Jr. She also served in that capacity from 1997 – 2006 under the leadership of Rev. Dr. James C. Wade, Jr. Deana currently holds a Bachelor's Degree in Elementary Education, an Associate's Degree in Marketing, and a Professional Certificate in Hotel Management and Travel. Deana's daughter Chareice has a Bachelor's and Master's Degrees in Psychology. Chareice coordinates the intake Program for Behavior

Health for Children and Teenagers in Georgia. She is currently pursuing her License in Professional Counseling (LPC). Chareice has one daughter, Sanai. For these reasons, having a love for children and being a part of a Children's Ministry is so important.

"We Have To Protect What We Advertise"

The size of your church does not determine your ministry; the effort put toward perfecting your ministry does. Perfection comes through the Power and Ministry of the Holy Spirit. The message has not changed, but our method has. Our method of motivating children in the past may not work today. All we have to do is look at the use of technologies. Jesus said that we would be able to do even "greater" things than He Himself did – in his humanity (St. John 14:12-14). Technology has opened up the world to us, but especially to young people. When used according to God's plan, what a great tool technology can play in motivating children to participate in ministry work. The question is: What is your method for perfecting the Children's Ministry, which God has called you to?

Many churches misuse the following premises for perfecting ministry work, possession, passion and perception.

1.   Possession
We think that the church is ours. We often think that the choir is ours, or whichever position we hold in the

ministry makes us owner. Jesus said, "Upon this rock I will build my church, and the gates of hell shall not prevail against it (Matthew 16:18).

2. Passion

We believe we have passion; yet, there is no real passion. We are unmoved in our ministry and we do it if we feel like it. We never go out of our way to really reach out to show someone we care, and if we do, it's only for a short period.

3. Perception

Many times, because we have a few children and at least some workers that come to Sunday School and church, we think everything is alright. We believe we are okay, but we are not.

The perfection of the ministry is summed up in the words of Jesus who said:

St. Matthews 19:14: *"But Jesus said, Suffer little children and forbid them not to come unto me, for of such is the kingdom of heaven."*

St. Luke 14:23, *"The Lord said, Go out into the highways and hedges and compel them to come in that my house may be filled."*

St. Matthews 28:18-20, *"All power is given unto me in heaven and in earth. (19) Go ye therefore and teach all nations, baptizing them in the name of the Father, and the Son, and of the Holy Ghost: (20) Teaching them to observe all things whatsoever I have commanded you. And lo, I am with you always, even unto the end of the world. Amen."*

"What about the Children? What about the Future?"

God wants us to give special attention to the children. When you reach out to help save children, you are actually saving your own future. The hope of a dying, hungry child is in a seed of faith. Your seed ensures a brighter future for them. Be compassionate. Don't ignore children; because they are our extension, and our future. We should feel fortunate having an opportunity to help make a child's dreams come true. This is the reason we must do something now. It is our responsibility to reach them and give them hope. Remember, every child is your child. What you make happen today, God will make happen for you.

There will never be enough children until every child is saved. Children are waiting for someone to tell them about Jesus, and it is our responsibility to get the message to them about our Lord and Savior Jesus Christ. Ella Wade's philosophy of Motivation is "We Must Never Forget God's Precious Children."

Chapter 6:
Methods for Teaching Children

Technological gadgets now dominate many aspects of our children's lives. We must realize that children are still looking for answers. Jesus Christ can only fill this void in their lives. A youth organization, which provides Christian Youth Ministry and Leadership resources puts it this way: "Youth need to know that God loves them, and that only through a personal relationship with the Lord Jesus Christ are they going to be able to experience the full extent of His love."

The methods we use to teach children need to be relevant to the experiences they face in their daily lives. However, we must be diligent in maintaining the Gospel of Jesus Christ, as we develop these methods. HOW (the method) we teach may change because generations and experiences do; however, the MESSAGE (Jesus Christ and Him Crucified) should never change.

The Lewis Center for Church Leadership in Washington D.C., lists below important methods, which can be used to strengthen ministry with youth:

- Honor the spirituality of youth.
- Equip parents to nurture their children's faith.
- "Get real" with Christian Education for youth.
- Provide excellent adult leadership for youth activities.
- Make worship meaningful for young persons.
- Create a sense of belonging for youth.

- Strive for effective youth fellowship.

One Lesson At A Time

Oftentimes, teaching children is not easy. In over 28 years as director of children's ministry, I have experienced working with children who are the same age but have varying abilities. Begin by teaching all children the same thing, to find out the most appropriate ability level to use. Children should never feel unwanted or unimportant. Use encouragement techniques with children at all times. Let them know that they are important and that they can do it.

Spend extra time with children who need it. Give difficult material to children who are more advance in learning. Drilling children over material given is one of the most effective ways to make sure they remember their parts. It is so important that the workers drill children over and over again until it gets into their spirit. Recruit the right staff and volunteers to assist with implementing your ideas.

A Director must be a Born-Again Christian that loves the Lord, loves the Pastor, loves the church, loves children, loves workers and loves children's parents.

Great Directors

- Are dedicated and committed to the Children's Ministry
- Are creative and present idea that are exciting and interesting for children

- Let children take an active role
- Teach songs that are fitting for children
- Know music or have some type of musical background
- Play an instrument (this would be helpful but not required)
- Participate in the Outreach Ministry
- Allow the children to participate in the Outreach Ministry to help witness to other children
- Never go to rehearsal unprepared
- Do not vent their frustration during rehearsal
- Are on time for rehearsal
- Greet the children
- Take an interest in children's school work
- Are Sunday School teachers
- Pray without ceasing

We must take into consideration that children learn by watching, listening, doing, or a combination of these three. Knowing how each child learns will help you develop programs that best serve each child individually.

No method you create for your Children's Ministry will work without prayer. Mark DeVries' has a book titled, *Sustainable Youth Ministry: Why Most Youth Ministry Doesn't Last and What Your Church Can Do about It*. He said, "Prayer is necessary for every aspect of youth ministry. The youth ministry should be saturated in prayer by a group of people who commit themselves to regular and aggressive prayer for every dimension of the ministry." It is important that children are taught the importance of prayer. We teach the following prayers to our children.

The Model Prayer: Matthew 6: 9-13

(9) After this manner therefore pray ye: Our Father which art in heaven, Hallowed be thy name (10) Thy kingdom come. Thy will be done in earth, as it is in heaven. (11) Give us this day our daily bread. (12) And forgive us our debts, as we forgive our debtors. (13) And lead us not into temptation but deliver us from evil: For thine is the kingdom, and the power, and the glory, forever Amen. (KJV)

A Prayer for Children 4 and Younger

Now lay me down to sleep

I pray the Lord my soul to keep

If I should die before I wake

I pray the Lord my soul to take

Bless mommy

Bless Daddy

Bless Me

Bless everybody, Amen.

A Prayer for Children 5 and Older

We thank you for this day.
Thank you for food on my table,
and clothes on my back.
Thank you for our Pastor (By name)
Thank you for our Pastor's wife (By name)
Thank you for everything.
And thank you for Jesus, Amen.

Sometimes while listening to prayer, the younger children didn't understand what the older children were saying. In their excitement, they would say, "Thank you Lord for food on my back and clothes on my table."

No method we use for teaching children will work until we realize that it is the Holy Spirit who changes lives; not us. Bringing children to Christ is a process, which takes time, commitment, love, and a focus on developing committed children who have a vision for sharing Christ.

Chapter 7:
The Qualifications and Requirements of Effective Workers

Assisting with the overall Vision

I cannot over-emphasize the importance of having effective workers involved in your youth ministry. Children are more easily influenced; therefore, it is imperative that children and youth workers possess and display Godly morals and values. It is not enough for these behaviors to be displayed only on Sundays, but it must be a part of their everyday lives. Ask the Lord in prayer to send workers who have a love for God and a love for children.

Children and youth workers should possess and display the following:

- A strong prayer life.
- a willing heart
- Patience and does not get tired of repeating the same message to children.
- Be familiar with all materials given by the Director.
- Maintain all material issued.
- Attend all activities, workshops and rehearsals.
- Attend all Children Ministry meetings.
- Be willing to sacrifice their time, talent, and treasure.
- Know the area in which she or he is best suited to work.
- Be willing to pick up the children if no transportation is available.

- Be on time for rehearsals and any planned programs for the children.
- Never leaves children unsupervised because things can happen in the blink of an eye.
- Memorize scriptures, songs or any material given in order to be prepared to teach the children.
- Assist with dressing the children at all times for all occasions.

We must continuously develop to be proficient in ministry. The quality of a person's character will reflect in his or her ministry work. Those of us who work in a children's ministry must strive to develop the skills God equips us with to do His will within the ministry. We must be willing to give God our best. He deserves nothing less. We must help our children grow spiritually and physically just as Jesus did. Luke 2:52 explain Jesus' growth, which is the model for the spiritual and physical growth of our children.

- He grew in Wisdom.
- He grew in Stature.
- He grew in favor with God.
- He grew in favor with Man.

We have to always keep in mind that these are the Lord's children and this is the Lord's work.

What Happens When There Are No Rules To Follow?

In II King 20:1 the Bible speaks about setting the house in order. *"Where there is no order, things become disorderly."*

There are rules and regulations in life we have to obey. In a Children's Ministry we have rules each child must follow. Approaching the importance of rules in a lackadaisical manner can be devastating to the ministry and those who are a part of it. There should also be appropriate consequences in place for children who break rules. However, workers must give them out in love and not anger. For this reason children workers must be loving, compassionate, and effective.

I. The effects on the ministry when rules are not in place:

      a. Chaos
      b. Confusion
      c. Lack of Order
      d. Lack of Unity
      e. Ineffectiveness

II. The results when rules are not followed:

      a. Parents may take their children out.
      b. Children are frustrated and smaller ones frightened.
      c. It is a turn off for new children joining the ministry

III. Consequences of children who do not follow the rules:

      a. Their behavior is reported to parents or guardians.
      b. They cannot sing or participate in other

activities.
c. They are not allowed to get special treats.
d. They cannot go on special outings.
e. They must be with an adult at all times.
f. They lose other privileges

IV. The results of having unqualified children workers in your ministry.

a. They become frustrated.
b. They let every little thing upset them.
c. They raise their voices when speaking to the children.
d. They complain about everything you present.
e. They lack interest in the children and the ministry.
f. Their patience is very thin.
g. They have a problem carrying out assignments.
h. They have a tendency to miss ministry meetings and rehearsals.
i. They cause division among other workers.
j. They don't familiarize themselves with materials, which results in poor teaching.

Worker Involvement

I encourage any ministry that is trying to reach a child now to setup an ADOPT-A-CHILD program. In this program adults care for a child as if he/she is their own. They agree to take on the responsibility of keeping up with a specific child to ensure their active involvement in the ministry. Adults who participate in the Adopt-A-Child program have supported children in several ways:

- Purchase uniforms when needed
- Visit the schools they attend
- Encourage them at all times
- Invite them to Sunday School
- Attend programs and other activities related to the child(ren)
- Visit their homes and get to know the parents
- Take time out to pray with and for them
- Attend Sunday School, and if possible, be a Sunday school teacher
- Attend intercessory prayer on Saturday morning at 10:00 a.m.
- Make contact with the child at least once a week.
- Schedule home visits as a follow up for children who repeatedly miss rehearsal and Sunday School

Worker Training

The most effective way to train workers is to conduct workshops.

- Workshops are designed for all workers to have the needed materials in advance.

- Workshops help prepare the workers and allow them to familiarize themselves with the material given in order to help the children.

- Workshops help workers understand which level of children they are best suited to work with.

- Workshops allow workers to get spiritually prepared for the Children's Ministry.

- Workshops are not only conducted to train workers, but for workers to learn how to work with each other in a Christian and loving atmosphere.

- Workshops are designed to equip the workers with prayer and the study and knowledge of the Word of God that they might impart the Word of God to the children.

- Workshops are conducted to help workers digest the vision that God has given the Pastor and Director, and to partner in the execution of the vision.

Chapter 8
Persuading Parents to Participate (The 3 P's)

Persuading Parents to Participate

It takes a village to raise a child, and we must start with the Parents. This area is so important because most of the children that are reached through the Outreach Ministry belong to parents that do not attend church. Since children possess great tenacity in not letting their parents, relatives or friends say no to them, they are quite effective in getting them to church to see them in action. If they have a solo, perform in a skit, read scriptures, praise dance, mime or whatever part they may have, children will ask repeatedly until the parents agree to come. When parents see their child perform and hear the Gospel they are presented with an opportunity to accept Christ as their own personal Savior.

Children can persuade parents to do almost everything imaginable because of the depth of a parent's love. Children have a way of tugging at your heart until you give in and say, yes.

- They persuade you to buy things you can't afford.

- They persuade you to let them go to different affairs when earlier you said, no.

- They persuade you to take them to McDonald's, even though you just cooked a full course meal.

Every parent (man or woman) was once a child.

If you take a look back over your life, you can say: Lord where would I be today if somebody had not taken the time to love me, nurture me and tell me about Jesus.

The Lord puts people in your life that will help you make it in life. I am talking from experiences I have had in my own life.

I had grandparents that I lived with, especially my grand-mother she took the time to love me, care for me, taught me how to pray, carried me to church, read the Bible before me and she let me know I could not make it without the Lord. We didn't have much but I knew that what they did for me was the best they could do.

Children, I want you to hear me today. You look at me now, but you don't know my story. I had to wear hand-me- down clothes and shoes. I had to eat food that my grandfather would get every day from the school where he worked that the white children didn't eat.

I thank God for the experience that I had as a child because it made me appreciate my parents more than ever. These experiences taught me that clothes, shoes, and material things don't determine what you will be in life. My grandmother's favorite word, which I will always remember, was "Jesus "all the time. I didn't understand then, but I do now. She was saying that Jesus is enough. Because of this I dedicated my life to work with the Children's Ministry to be a blessing to other children.

I am telling you this because I see how children get attitudes and become upset when they can't get what they want. Children need to thank God for having parents that love them enough to give them some of the things they ask for.

In this same house where I lived there were rules. We could not do any and everything, like talk back, roll our eyes, or smack our lips in anger. Honey, that was a definite, NO-NO!

I smarted off to my grandmother one time, and before I could get it out of my mouth I had a mark on my face, from a wet towel in her hand, (you know one of those back hand licks) that taught me a great lesson. Never again did she see me even look like I didn't like what she said.

I thank God that my grandmother loved me enough to let me know that she took care of me, and I was not to disrespect her. She was quick to say, "I will help take you out of here."

Below is a true account of an incident, which took place with my granddaughter Brishonda and her son Braylen.

One morning, our granddaughter and great-grandson son who lives with us most of the time was making preparation to take him to school. As usual she runs late. I called her in the bedroom and gave her some helpful advice to keep her from being late every day.

Of course she did not receive what I was saying, and stormed out the room with an attitude. I said loudly something bad is going to happen to you, because you have a terrible attitude this morning. She made no reply to me, but told her son to get in the car. I told my husband that something bad was going to happen to our granddaughter because of the way she was acting.

So we begin to pray for her. Not two minutes later while we were praying the telephone rang, but I didn't answer it because we were praying. The phone rang again and we stopped praying, I told Rev. Wade that I bet it was Brishonda. I answered and just like I said it was Brishonda just had an accident just that quick, one block from the house. She was hysterical, mama can you come down here I just hit a car, what am I going to do. I politely told her call the police and I'll be there when I get up and put my clothes on. I took my time and went to the site.

The policeman had already arrived and Braylen was all over the place telling the story about how his mother had bruised the man's car, and hit it so hard until the policeman had to smile. I told the officer I wanted to get Braylen to school because he was already late, and I left her there to handle the situation on her own.

From that day until this very day, Brishonda has never tried that again. It was a great lesson for her on learning to respect and listen to your parents.

We are in a Battle to Save Our Children

If our children are to be saved, they must be taught the Plan of Salvation, which is mentioned in an earlier chapter. It's in the Word.

Romans 10: 9-10

(9)That if thou shalt confess with thy mouth the Lord Jesus, and shalt believe in thine heart that God hath raised him from the dead, thou shalt be saved. (10)For with the heart man believeth unto righteousness; and with the mouth confession is made unto salvation.

St. John 3:16-17

(16) For God so loved the world that he gave his only begotten son that whosoever believeth in him should not perish but have everlasting life. (17) For God sent not his son into the world to condemn the world, but that the world through him might be saved."

I want all parents and children to know that Satan, Lucifer, which is the Devil, is out to destroy our children, tear up our homes and wreck our families. St. John 10:10 says, "*The thief (*that's the Devil, Satan) *cometh, not but for to steal, and to kill, and to destroy.* But this is what the Lord says, "*I am come that they might have life, and that they might have it more abundantly."*

Children must be taught the Biblical principle of obeying their parents. Stop listening to what somebody else says. Living with your parents, eating the foot they buy, wearing the clothes they buy, sleeping in their bed, driving their cars, spending their money, but listening and following somebody else?

Children must be taught to be Obedient

Ephesians 6:1-3 says, *(1) "Children obey your parents in the Lord for this is right. (2)Honor thy father and mother; which is the first commandment with promise; (3) That it may be well with thee, and thou mayest live long on the earth."*

We are in a Struggle

One of the reasons that the struggle is so difficult is that we are have gotten away from Christian morals and values. There is no respect, and children say what they want to say. (Talk back to their parents and other adults; saying yea, yep, and naw instead of Yes or No. Yes, Ma'am and No, Sir are foreign languages that nobody speaks today.

Man wants you to Negotiate and Rationalize values. You do not have to negotiate with your children. If you tell your child to do something, then that settles it.

This is a Strange Generation:

Our young people today have attitude, but no aptitude (no intelligence, talent). They are dressed to kill and killing to dress.

We buy our children things when we know we are struggling with our finances.

What are Some Answers for Parents?

- Tell children the truth. If you don't have what they ask for, "Be For Real."
- Stop getting in debt trying to please children to keep them happy.
- Stop letting children make important decisions?
- Stop doing your own thing and give some quality time to your children.
- Children should not have the responsibility of babysitting the children, preparing meals, and keeping the house while you are out or not in the mood to handle it yourself.
- Children should not become their own boss.

Parenting can be one of the most difficult, yet rewarding experiences you can have in your lifetime. Children are a blessing from God and He puts the responsibility of receiving and raising them on us.

- Parent spends quality time with your child (children).
- A hug or a kind word have lasting effects on children.
- Encourage them; let your child know that he or she is going to make it, and that you are

proud of them.
- Visit the school to see what your child is doing.
- Help with their homework.
- Eat together
- Pray together
- Bring your child to church so you can worship together.
- Talk to your Children about the things that are happening all around them.

Matthew 18:5 says, *"And whoever shall receive one such little child in my name receiveth me."*

In Proverbs 22:6 we find the words, *"Train up a child in the way he should go: and when he is old he will not depart from it."*

Raising children takes love, sacrifice, and commitment, but nothing but the Word of God (The Bible) will bring deliverance for them from a world, which places more value on gaining material wealth than living a life, which is pleasing to the Lord.

How To Get Parents To Participate:

- Be patient when you knock on the door.
- Bo pleasant and friendly when you speak to the parents.
- Keep your visitation short.
- When visiting parents your approach should

be:
1. Greeting
2. Your name
3. Pastor's name
4. Name of your church
5. Purpose of your visit
6. Share in a brief prayer and scripture
7. Invite the parents, as well as their children.
8. Get the proper information from the mother, father or guardian.
9. Inform parents that they should be responsible for getting the children to and from rehearsals. If this is not possible, the Bus Ministry is available to assist with transportation needs.

I cannot stress more strongly the importance of approaching parents to be active and participate with their children in ministry work. As children ministry leaders we must be diligent in persuading parents to participate. Jesus said compel, so we must compel them with all diligence.

Chapter 9:
The Sustainability of Workers: Staying with a Children's Ministry

The Importance of Consistency when it comes to Children

There is only one way to stay with the Children's Ministry, and it is by the precious Blood of the Lamb. You have to learn how to depend on Jesus. When God anoints you for ministry, He always gives you the staying power.

You stay because this is a commission from God, given to the man of God, for the people of God to impart to the children of God. You stay because you are helping some child know about Jesus Christ.

You stay because you were a child and somebody took the time to love you and care enough to show you the way to Jesus Christ. You stay because you have the promise of Jesus.

Matthew 28:19-20
"Therefore, go and "make disciples" of all the nation, baptizing them in the man of the Father, and the Son, and of the Holy Spirit. (20)Teach these new disciples to obey all the commands I have given you. And be sure of this: I am with you always, even to the end of the age." (NLT)

Hebrews 13:5
"I will never leave thee, nor forsake thee."

Special Challenges

One of my challenges as Director of the Children's Ministry, which made me determined to keep going was seeing how God renewed my strength.

Philippians 4:13 says, *"I can do all things Christ which strengthens me."*

I have quoted this scripture many times when I felt I had no strength. (And the Lord knows that we get tired and weak along the way). It is during these times that I am reminded from where all of my strength comes from. The strength that I am talking about is not finite; it is strength that only comes from our Infinite God. Through Christ we are able to do all things. There were days when I felt like I had had enough and could not go on, but somehow, someway, the Lord stepped in at that very moment. When you surrender and call on the name of Jesus; He will come to see about you, He will renew your strength.

Isaiah 40:31
"But they that wait on the Lord shall renew their strength; they shall mount up with wings as eagles; they shall run, and not be weary, they shall walk and not faint."

Spiritual Growth and Development from the Children's Ministry

In addition to growing in age and stature, children in the ministry also grow spiritually through bible reading, songs and stories about Jesus. Many accept Christ as their personal Savior while they are members of the Children's choir.

The Following are areas in which they develop:

Drill Team Ministry

Praise Team Ministry

Mime Ministry

Memorizing scripture, including the Church's Mission and Vision

Plays and Skills

Playing Instruments

Recitation and Public Speaking

Discipline

Plan of Salvation

Respect for Pastor, Church, Parents, Adults and Each other

New Talents

Workshops

Outings

Singing at other churches and events

Chapter 10:
A Tribute to Greatness

"God is not unjust; He will not forget your work and the love you have shown Him as you have helped his people and continue to help them" (Hebrews 6:10).

What a humbling experience to be in the presence of true greatness! For 28 years, I have had the opportunity to watch the example of someone committed to what she does, not just at the beginning but also throughout the entire process. She did it not because of who she is, but for whom she belongs. Twenty-eight years is a long time to do anything! People come and go situations and people change, but to remain unwavering in dedication and purpose throughout this time is the mark of true passion and professionalism.

A professional is someone who follows a line of conduct, characterized by conforming to ethical standards in a conscientious and generally business-like manner. To be passionate is to be enthusiastic, ardent, and full of zeal "an unflagging pursuit of an aim or devotion to a cause." Mrs. Ella Wade has demonstrated these characteristics consistently over these 28 years. She has not faltered or lost step in the passion to save lives through song.

"But Jesus said, Suffer little children, and forbid them not, to come unto me: for such is the Kingdom of Heaven." St. Matthew 19:14

Mrs. Ella Wade has taught, guided, directed, loved (children) individually for who they are, and prayed for over 3000 children. She has also encouraged, taught, cajoled, praised and most of all prayed for the parents, grandparents and guardians of these children. Workers and bus drivers that were initially ill equipped for the task before them were presented with an example of a servant who managed, directed, supported and prayed for them.

Hundreds, maybe thousands, of songs taught; scores written; plays written, designed and directed; and budding talent discovered, developed and nurtured were always, consistently done with a gentle, humble and long suffering spirit.

Thank you Mrs. Wade,

- **Your Member,** *Yvonne Sanders*

"Giving thanks always for all things unto God and the Father in the name of our Lord Jesus Christ" (Ephesians 5:20).

Words cannot express my gratitude to this "Elegant Woman of God," Sis. Ella M. Wade. This godly woman has been an extension of my mother for thirty plus years. Now that my mother has gone on to be with the Lord, Sis. Ella M. Wade is my mother.

A woman that took me under her wings and help mold me into the young adult Christian woman that I am today. A woman that literally helped me raise my daughter, Chareice, from birth, and is now 30 years old. I thought so much of Sis. Ella Wade that my daughter's middle name is "Ella."

Mrs. Wade is a musically gifted and talented musician, who taught me so much about the music ministry. A woman who led the Zion Missionary Baptist Church's 100 Voice Plus Children's Choir for 28 years, molding thousands of children and manifesting musical talents in children and adults that they were not even aware of. She is a dedicated, committed, faithful and loyal wife, sister, mother, grandmother, great grandmother, friend, and confidante.

If there was one scripture that could define her it would be Proverbs 31:10, *"Who can find a virtuous woman? For her price is far above rubies"*

I Love You So Much!

- **Your daughter, *Deana M. Johnson***
-

As a parent, I wanted my children to experience all that I did not as a child growing up in the church. Proverbs 22: 6 says, *"Train up a child in the way he should go: and when he is old, he will not depart from it."* So, when my three children were potty-trained, they became active members in Zion's 100 Plus voice Children's Choir. My son Maurice, who is now 29 years old, says he remembers discipline, long rehearsals, and lots of practice. My daughter LaShanna, who is now 26 years old, says she remembers discipline and organization; and my daughter Shannon, the oldest who is now 32 years old, says she remembers discipline and perfection. They all had one common thing they remembered and that was discipline. They didn't have an appreciation for discipline as children, but as adults they now understand and appreciate that discipline led to things being structured, as God requires us to do things decent and in order.

I Corinthians 3: 6 says, *"I have planted, Apollos watered; but God gave the increase."* As a result of the good seeds planted at home and in Zion's 100 Plus Voice Children's Choir, not only did my children sing about Jesus and his goodness, they were taught about who Jesus is and how important it is to have him in their lives. As children, they were taught that practice makes perfect, how to work with others, how to listen and follow instructions, how to be and do your best, to never give up, and most importantly, how to love God first and to love your neighbor as yourself. On their own accord, because of the good seeds planted, each of my children at the age of four asked to be baptized and as adults are active members planting good seed through various ministries at their respective churches.

The lessons learned in Zion's 100-Plus Voice Children's Choir are lifelong lessons and because of them, we have been truly blessed.

Former member of Zion Missionary Baptist Church, and currently the first lady of New Tabernacle M. B. Church in Gary, Indiana where her husband, Rev. Chet J. Johnson, Sr., is Pastor.

- **Sharon L. Johnson**

As I reflect back on the yester-years, the 100 Plus Voice Children's Choir were a weekly regiment and a way of life for my three children. Of course my children looked forward to connecting with their friends, sharing snacks, having a good time all while learning about Jesus and loving every minute of it.

Under the direction of Sister Ella Wade, a very diligent, dedicated, and devoted servant of God, her love for God was apparent and very transparent. She kept the children excited, challenged. They were honored to be a part of the 100-Plus Voice Children's Choir, representing on the local and state levels. Sister Wade taught the children to pray, sing, dance, and the importance of worship. There is absolutely no doubt in my mind that the prayers, songs, and scripture readings have greatly attributed to the growth and development of my now, three adult children.

As a single mother, I am grateful to the Lord; my mommy, Willie Maude Glover; Pastor Wade; Sister Wade; and the 100 Plus Voice Children's Choir for helping to lay a good foundation that will carry my amazing children for the rest of their lives.

Continued blessings and success as you continue to walk in our anointing in helping the babies, which you love so much.

Former member who grew up in Zion MISSIONARY BAPTIST Church, and raised her three children at Zion.

- Renee Glover

The time is so appropriate for writing this book. Women of all ethnic groups are being recognized and honored for their accomplishments, both nationally and internationally.

Locally and throughout the Midwest Region, the reality of the vision given to Rev. James Commodore Wade, Jr. Emeritus and Mrs. Ella M. Wade Emerita will be long remembered.

The 100 Plus Voice Children's Choir has celebrated for 28 years under the leadership of Mrs. Ella M. Wade and now 4 years later, God is still blessing this awesome ministry.

Each year people from near and far have looked forward to this celebration, and have been amazed by not only the number of children in the choir, but by the outstanding talent, professionalism and spirit-filled musical they experience. However, none of this could have been possible without God's presence.

Although the members of the 100-Plus Voice Children's Choir are not her biological children, Mrs. Ella Wade and her workers realize that: What they know, they taught them. Where they are, they brought them, and where they go, they must show them the way!

Over 3000 Children and 32 years later, Zion, you can be proud, and we can boast that under the leadership of Mrs. Ella M. Wade and her workers. We have young people who work in more than 24 career fields.

- Patricia Dixon-Darden

A Dedicated Worker

By Mrs. Camellia P. Wade-McKinley

I had the wonderful opportunity and pleasure of working with Mrs. Wade and the Zion Missionary Baptist Church's 100 Voice Children's Choir for 12 years as a Worker and Music Director. The experience and knowledge acquired under her tutelage has been rewarding in both my Christian and professional career.

Mrs. Wade has a firm but gentle approach. She has "mastered" teaching children to enjoy singing, as well as encouraging them to strive for excellence and perfection. Working with her has reinforced the importance and significance of Giving God your best through time and your talent. Mrs. Wade believes in "looking and sounding good." Because of Christ and through the example portrayed by Mrs. Wade, I have been able to successfully serve as a Children's Ministry Director and teach music in all grades in the East Chicago, Indiana and Dallas, Texas school systems.

The unwavering love and affection exhibited by Mrs. Wade is remarkable. What is most significant in my memories of working with Mrs. Wade and the 100 Voice Children's Choir is the commitment she disclosed and the desire from those who shared in the Children's Ministry with her. She believes every child is special! And for this cause she instructed us to reach out and "Save the Children."

Thank you Mrs. Wade for sharing your gift with me, it is cherished! God Bless you as you feast on the harvest you have planted.

Having the opportunity and blessing of studying and gaining knowledge under Sis. Ella Wade was not only given to me, but to my daughter as well. My daughter *Sabrina Ella McKinley,* is named in honor of my mother. Sabrina was given the opportunity to sing in the 100 Plus Voice Children's Choir where she learned to sing soprano, along with the importance of scripture, church etiquette, discipline, and tithing. Self-respect and love were also reinforced. In addition, Sabrina was given the wonderful opportunity to share in the awesome praise dance ministry, where she learned to praise God through theatrical movement. Words cannot express the blessings Sabrina has gained by having a God-filled grandmother who shared her gifts and love.

A Dedicated Worker

By Mrs. LaShonta J. Thompson

Having the opportunity and blessing of studying and gaining knowledge under Sis. Wade was not only given to me, but to my daughter as well. My daughter, Sabrina Ella, who is named after my mother, attended the Zion Academic Academy, which was originally named the ZBC Nursery School where Mrs. Wade served as Director for 17 years.

Sabrina was given the opportunity to sing in the 100-Plus Voice Children's Choir where she learned to sing soprano, along with the importance of scripture, church etiquette, discipline and tithing. Self-respecting and love were also reinforced! In addition, Sabrina was given the wonderful opportunity to share in the awesome praise dance ministry where she learned to praise God through theatrical movement. Words cannot express the blessings Sabrina has gained by having a God-filled grandmother who shared her gifts and love.

Being in the home of a Pastor and his wife, where attending church was not an option, the true meaning of God's Word became evident which reads: *"Train up a child in the way he should go and when he is old he will not depart from it"* (Proverbs 22:6).

At the age of four, I began singing in the Children's Choir of Zion known as the Cherubs. By the age of ten, I began singing in the Children's Choir under the leadership of my father, Rev. Dr. J.C. Wade, Jr., and the direction of my mother, Sis. Ella Wade. Through this ministry, I grew spiritually in various ways; learning scriptures, the importance of prayer, the plan of salvation, and Christian discipleship. Also, the Children's Choir Ministry was a musical enhancement through constant development of ear training, intonation, diction, vocal control and spiritual expression through music.

In 2009, while serving as Assistant Director, God allowed me to sit under the tutelage of Sis. Ella Wade as God gave her continued wisdom to direct over 100 children. I was able to learn steps for evangelism in Children's Ministry, how to formulate programs for children, and develop techniques to both capture and sustain the enthusiasm of children.

"But as it is written, eyes hath not seen, nor ear heard, neither have entered into the heart of man, the things which God hath prepared for them that love Him" (I Corinthians 2:9).

Today, nearly thirty-five years later, God has blessed me to share in ministry at Zion M. B. C. as Director of the Children's Ministry under the leadership of my husband, Rev. Dr. Charles L Thompson, Jr.

"Now unto him that is able to so exceedingly abundantly above all that we ask or think, according to the power that worketh in us, Unto Him be glory in the church by Christ Jesus throughout all ages, world without end. Amen" (Ephesians 3:20-21).

And now our children, *Charles Lee Thompson, III and Cameron James Thompson* are proud to be the grandchildren of Rev. and Mrs. Wade, and the Zion Missionary Baptist Church Children's Choir Ministry. Because of this awesome ministry and vision, we are blessed in many ways.

Over 50 Years of Friendship
Tribute from Dr. & Mrs. Samuel J. Gilbert Sr.

Grace be unto you and peace, from our God and father, and from the Lord Jesus Christ. I thank my God upon every remembrance of you, always in every prayer of mine for you all making request with joy."

Philippians 1:2-4

<u>Simple Steps to Reach Each Child Now</u> is a must read book for all those that work with children. The author of this book is well prepared in teaching us how to reach our children at home, church and abroad through a children's ministry.

We have seen the lessons Mrs. Ella Wade learned from her early upbringing impact her own children. We have been with the Wade's through all their challenges faced, and all of the successes they have enjoyed. We have been with them in times of disappointment and celebrations in victories. We know their relationship with God through prayer. We have been influenced greatly by observing their daily habit of prayer and meeting with God on their knees, in their prayer closet, and praying with friends like us.

There is a subtle attack taking place on <u>our families</u> today like never before. Satan is out to destroy our <u>future generation</u> with emphasis on destroying a people of faith. Satan uses the <u>art of deception</u> to lure our children in all kinds of ungodly behaviors. In the book of Ephesians, Paul warned us to put on "<u>the whole armor of God</u>, that we might be able to stand against the <u>wiles</u> of the devil" (Eph. 6:11). Satan cannot attack us outright because we belong to God, and we are in His hands, but he does everything he can to draw us away from God.

Children <u>need a fresh touch</u> from God our father and the lord Jesus Christ, and a determination that God's plan will not be defeated.

Simple Steps to Reach Each Child Now will help us on our journey. We highly recommend this book for your children's ministry, which will help them in their physical, cultural, economic and spiritual development.

Mrs. Ella Wade not only instructs us in this book, but she has lived it in her own life. My prayer is that this book will bring new insight and strategies that will cause our children to be victorious in the name of Christ.

Tribute to my Sister

The love, joy and pride that I have for my sister Mrs. Ella Wade runs deep. We have shared many memorable years together, her gift of kindness and ability to share with others is how I remember her, She always used her talent in music even as a child.

The children's ministry at Zion Baptist Church was her joy, for many years I would hear her say I am on my way to the children's choir rehearsal, it was always something about the children.

The love, care, knowledge, teaching and spiritual growth that each child received is a true blessing.

Simple Steps to Reach Each Child Now is a result of years of prayer, patience, perseverance and persistence. It is truly a pleasure to extend congratulation and best wishes to you my sister on this exciting accomplishment in your life, I am honored to be your sister.

This milestone reflects the spiritual leadership you have provided for Zion Missionary Baptist Church.

Your Loving Sister,

- **Mrs. Alice Faye Stanton**

A Tribute to Lady Tiffany Nicole Collins Smith

The name Tiffany in Greek is Theophaneia, which means Vision of God. Her name bespeaks of her Mission and Ministry for this book:

"Simple Steps to Reach Each Child Now", and the book written by my husband Rev. Dr. James C. Wade Jr. "Not Too Early Not Too Late " (Life After Retirement). To her legacy she exposed these books on the eve of her death through social media (twitter & face book). By exposing these books she knew it would be a blessing to those who have a love for Children's Ministry, Pastors, Ministers and for the body of Christ. You were a beacon light for young Christian women and the Christian world. In your walk with God, you would often tell me that if I am to pursue a goal in my life it must reflect my desire to understand and give God my all.

Humbly Submitted,

- **Mrs. Ella Mae Wade**

Chapter 12:
Generations Speaks

Four Generations of 100-Plus Voice Children's Choir

The 100 Voice Children's Choir has been a "family affair" at Zion. Like the Wade Family, The Upshaw Family has also been a part of the 100 Voice Children's Choir for four generations.

FIRST GENERATION
Freddie L. Upshaw

Mrs. Freddie L. Upshaw, deceased family matriarch, was blessed to have her daughter, Delincia; granddaughter, Tailiah; and now great-grandchildren; Derea, Clifford and Darion, as a part of the children's choir. Inspired and motivated by her mentors and friends, Rev. Dr. James Commodore Wade, Jr. and Mrs. Ella M. Wade, Mrs. Upshaw began working with the children's choir in 1983 and served for nine years, until 1992. Allowing her light to shine everywhere she went, Ms. Upshaw was dedicated, kind, gentle and concerned. Being a worker was a blessed privilege for her.

SECOND GENERATION
100-Plus Voice Children's Choir, Former Member
Delincia Upshaw Smith

The 100-Plus Voice Children's Choir was a major part of my Christian growth and maturity. I don't know where I would be in my life today without the foundation that the choir provided from the early age of five to until I became a teenager. I didn't always want to attend choir rehearsal but my parents were adamant about my going. Looking back over my life, I'm glad and appreciate they made me attend. I started out as a choir member and was promoted to a Children's Choir Junior Worker, which instilled a sense of responsibility and mentorship by becoming a role model for the younger generation.

Not only did I learn to sing God's praises, but I also learned that Jesus loved me unconditionally, and that *"I can do all things through Christ which strengthen me"* (Philippians 4:13).

I learned how to pray and that prayer changes things; how to lift up the name of Jesus; and how to honor my parents and respect my peers. My mother and Mrs. Ella Wade encouraged me to recite bible verses and participate in plays, which sharpened my communication and leadership skills. These skills have helped me today in my chosen career because I am not fearful of speaking publicly.

I can still remember my first solo; "All God's Children" and the first time I had to narrate a song entitled "I Am a Promise." Some of the songs that I learned in the Children's Choir helped me to get through many trials, tribulations, and obstacles throughout my life. These songs of praises encouraged me to remain steadfast, unmovable, always abounding in the work of the Lord and those songs still live in me today. Thank God for the wisdom my parents had to send me to choir rehearsal, the vision of Rev. and Mrs. Wade and the support of the

Zion Missionary Baptist Church family to provide a place for children to not only sing God's praises but to grow in the Lord.

THIRD GENERATION
100-Plus Voice Children's Choir, Former Member
Tailiah D. Morris

Being a part of the 100 Voice Children's Choir has been a tremendous blessing in my life. Four generations of my family have come through the choir and I can say without a doubt that it is a family heirloom that is priceless. There is no dollar amount that you can ever put on the experience and teaching that comes from being a member of this great choir. It's more than just singing and learning songs. For most kids it's their first encounter with Jesus Christ.

The choir also helps to develop social skills, learning skills, proper behavior and etiquette as well as morals. This is the greatest foundation for any child. My children, Clifford, Darea, and Darion, who are now in the 100 Plus Voice Children's Choir say they love to sing, as well as participate in the different activities within the choir. *"Train up a child in the way he should go and when he is old he will not depart from it" (Proverbs 22:6).*

What better way to train up a child than in the Children's Choir? When obstacles and trials come their way, they can remember the teachings that they have learned from the choir as I have had to so many times.

SECOND GENERATION

The son of Rev. Dr. J.C. and Mrs. Ella Wade, Jr.
Rev. James Commodore Wade III.

As a young boy, I was baptized, ordained, and licensed to preach the word of God by my father, Rev. Dr. James C. Wade, Jr.

I am blessed with the gift of music; I played the drums and the guitar for the children's choir. At an early age, my siblings and I were taught how to sing and were given music lessons to enhance our gifts in music by our mother. There were days when my mother and I were the only musicians; I played the drums and guitar and she was on the organ.

I thank God for a mother who taught us to love the Lord and give Him our best.

THIRD AND FORTH GENERATIONS

Granddaughter, and Great-grandson of Rev. Dr. J.C. and Mrs. Ella Wade, Jr.
Brishonda and Braylen.

When I started with the 100-Plus Voice Children's Choir I was just two years old. I was a 3rd generation member. I was just learning how to really talk while learning to sing and quote scriptures. I didn't know anything about three-part harmony or trying to hold a note. I was just a little girl who was in the children's choir not because I wanted to, but because I had to. I never knew the importance that it would have on my life until I got a little older.

Growing up I saw my grandmother, Mrs. Ella Wade, along with the workers work with hundreds of hardheaded, busy children including myself. No matter how mischievous or hardheaded I was, they never gave up on me. My grandmother not only put a lot of time into me at church, she also worked with me at home. Mrs. Wade taught me songs, scriptures, and scripts. She even taught us as children how to put on a whole production.

In addition to learning how to sing, I learned how to carry myself with dignity, how to respect others, and most of all, how to love God and be a Christian. Eventually, I was going to choir because I wanted to not because I had to. Just the opportunities that I was able to experience were irreplaceable and unexplainable. I could have never imagined life without that experience which has helped to groom me into the woman that I am today. The 100 Voice Children's Choir ministry is definitely a firm believer of Proverbs 22:6 *"Train up a child in the way he should go, And when he is old he will not depart from it."*

My son, Braylen, is a 4th generation 100 Voice Children's Choir member. He started when he was two and he is now seven. Just seeing how he has grown from then until now just brings joy to my heart. I am able to see my son have the same experience and opportunities in life that I had. At the age of seven he is growing more spiritually every day. I encourage all parents to get their children in the children's choir. I will never know the impact that this is going to have on my son later on in life. However, as he grows up to be a young Christian man, he will know that there are better things in life than being on the streets, because only what you do for Christ will last.

About the Author
Mrs. Ella M. Wade

Mrs. Ella M. Wade was born March 20, 1941 in Daingerfield, Texas to Azilee Turner and Ike Hodge. She accepted Christ at the age of 7 during a Sunday service at New Hope Baptist Church, Pastor Rev. Otis Warren. As a child Mrs. Wade served as one of New Hope Baptist Church musician during that time.

She graduated from J.J. Rhodes High School in Dangerfield, Texas with honors. After graduation she attended Bishop College in Marshall, Texas with a 4 year Music scholarship in Band. Her area of expertise was a flute major. She was a member of the Coledridge Taylor Choral Society Choir until the school moved to Dallas, Texas.

January 27th, 1963 she was united in Holy Matrimony to Rev. Dr. James Commodore Wade Jr. They were married at the Samaria Baptist Church. Van Alstyne Texas. This begins the legacy of the Rev. Dr. James Commodore Wade, Jr. and Mrs. Ella M. Wade. She was a substitute teacher at the Van Alstyne Elementary School in Van Alstyne, Texas and served as musician for Samaria Baptist Church, in Van Alstyne Texas and later at the Pilgrim Rest Baptist Church Van Buren, Arkansas. In 1964 their first child was born, James Commodore Wade, III.

In February 1965, Rev. Dr. Wade Jr. was called to Pastor the Zion Missionary Baptist Church in East Chicago, Indiana with his wife Mrs. Wade and son. In 1968 God blessed them with their second child; a daughter Camellia P. Wade - (McKinley) and in 1972 their third child was born; a daughter, LaShonta J. Wade (Thompson).

During her tenure at Zion, she traveled to Israel with her husband for extensive studies specializing in Biblical and Theological principals.

For 45 years, she ministered with her husband at Zion Missionary Baptist Church, served as Minister of Music for eighteen years, Director of Children's Ministry for 28 years, Director of Z.B.C Nursery School (which was later named Zion Academic Academy), co- founder with her husband for the Prevention and Drug Awareness After School Tutorial Program, served with the outreach "In Reach Ministry" and Bus Ministry.

She served as President of General Missionary Baptist State Convention of Indiana, Matron Auxiliary, Musician and Director of the "Youth Explosion" under the leadership of Rev. Dr. James Commodore Wade, Jr. Presidency.

Mrs. Wade also conducted the Children's Workshops in the following churches:

- Frankfort, Germany, Rev. Smith, Pastor, Zion Baptist Church

- Ft. Lauderdale FL, Dr. Mack King Carter, Pastor, Olive Baptist Church

- Sana Ana, California, Rev. George Banks, Pastor, Graceland Community Baptist Church

- Gary, Indiana, Rev. Chet J. Johnson, Sr., New Tabernacle Baptist Church

- East Chicago, Indiana, Rev. Kelly B. Williams Sr., Pastor, Greater Destiny Bible Church, Provide annual children's ministry training, Mrs. Ella M. Wade is also first lady Emerita of Greater Destiny Bible Church, in addition to Zion Missionary Baptist Church.

- St. Croix, Virgin Island, Rev. Will Woods, Pastor, Altone Baptist Church

- Los Angeles, California, Rev. Dr. Melvin Von Wade Sr., Pastor, Mount Moriah Baptist Church

- East Chicago, Indiana, Zion Missionary Baptist Church, Rev. Dr. James C. Wade Jr., Pastor, Conduct Children's Workshop

- St. Paul Minnesota, Shiloh Missionary Church, Rev. Dr. Steve Daniels, Pastor Women of the Word Conference (WOW)

She conducted a Women's Conference at the National Baptist Association of Germany and a keynote speaker for Women of the Word Conference (WOW) in St. Paul Minnesota. The majority of her career includes substitute teaching at various grammar schools, of which Maywood Elementary school in Hammond, Indiana and McKinley Elementary School, East Chicago IN.

Mrs. Wade assisted with the Children's Ministry at Mount Moriah Missionary Baptist Church in Los

Angeles, California for four months under the leadership of Rev. Dr. Melvin Von Wade. The partial fulfillment of the vision of Pastor Wade and Mount Moriah MISSIONARY BAPTIST Church family occurred at their Annual Children's Day. There were 66 children in attendance, and under the anointing of the Holy Spirit 22 souls came to Christ.

Mrs. Wade states that she is grateful to God because of the united effort of those who worked in the Children's Ministry at Mount Moriah. She is thankful for the privilege of working with Pastor Melvin Wade Sr., Yvonne James, Minister of Music; April Williams, Mattie Handy, James Goodlow, and others who shared in the Children's Ministry.

On April 19, 2009 a scholarship was set up named Mrs. Ella M. Wade Scholarship Fund in the amount of $500.00 from the 100 Plus Voice Children's Choir Anniversary, plus $500.00 supplemented by Mrs. Wade, which would total $1,000.00. This Scholarship will be given to one student in the amount of $1,000.00 of two students in the amount of $500.00 each.

She traveled to Oxford, England three times with her husband to Proclaimers Place at Oxford University for Extended Biblical Studies. In her lifetime she has visited over 30 Countries. She attended Indiana University Northwest, Gary Indiana. She completed her Bachelors of Theology in Religious Education at GMOR Theological Institute, Gary, Indiana. In 2011, she received an Honorary Doctoral in Sacred and Gospel Music, Global Evangelical Christian College and Seminary, Wetumpka, Alabama. Mrs. Wade just completed a three night Institute Commitment Workshop Revival with her husband.

Mrs. Wade now serves as Executive Consultant to the Music Ministry under the leadership of our Pastor, Rev. Dr. Charles L. Thompson II. Mrs. Wade presently resides with her husband in East Chicago, IN. She is the proud mother of one son, Rev. James Commodore Wade III, two daughters, Camellia Patrice McKinley (Rev. Dr. Thomas McKinley) and LaShonta Jenene Thompson (Rev. Dr. Charles L Thompson II). Two granddaughters, Brishonda Dotrice Wade and Sabrina Ella McKinley, two grand-sons Charles L. Thompson III and Cameron J. Thompson and one great-grandson Braylen Chafen.

Mrs. Wade is a born again child of God, who loves the Lord with all her heart, mind, soul and strength. She is known for her love, dedication, commitment and spiritual leadership in Children's Ministry. Her favorite scripture verse is: *"O Lord, our Lord, how excellent is thy name in all the Earth, who hast set they glory above the Heavens"* (Psalms 8:1).

"And this is the confidence that we have in him, that, if we ask any thing according to his will, he heareth us: And if we know that he hear us, whatsoever we ask, we know that we have the petitions that we desired of him" (I John 5:14-15).

Made in the USA
Columbia, SC
07 April 2019